While You Were Sleeping

John Butler

PEACHTREE

ATLANTA

For Daisy and Kate

Ω
Published by
PEACHTREE PUBLISHERS, LTD.
1700 Chattahoochee Avenue
Atlanta, Georgia 30318-2112

www.peachtree-online.com

Text and illustrations © 1996 by John Butler

First published by Orchard Books in Great Britain, 1999.

Printed in Singapore

10 9 8 7 6 5 4 3 2

Cataloging-in-Publication for this book is available from the Library of Congress

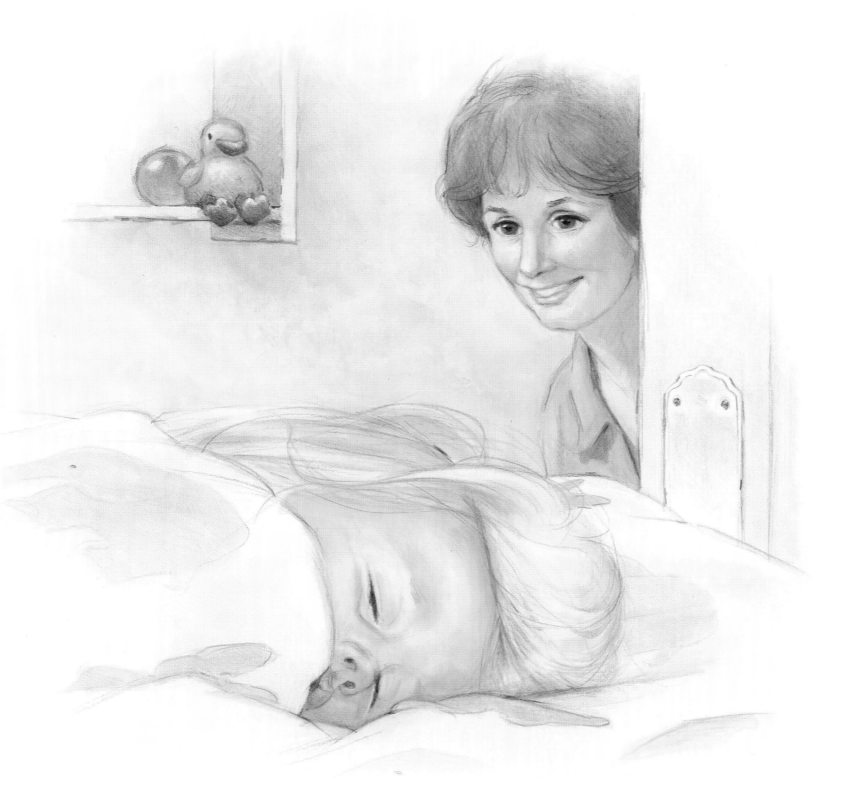

"Wake up, Daisy," said her mother.
She gave Daisy a good morning kiss.

"Is it time to get up?" said Daisy.

"Yes. The sun is shining," said her mother, "and the animals that were awake last night have gone to bed now."

"What were they doing while I was sleeping?" asked Daisy.

"Well," her mother said,…

"while you were sleeping,
one tiger went hunting in the jungle,

and while you were sleeping,
two mice made a warm,
cozy nest in the hay.

While you were sleeping,
three bears played
chase in the snow,

and while you were sleeping, four baby owls
sat wide-eyed in an old oak tree.

While you were sleeping, five dolphins
leapt out of the deep, blue sea,

and while you were sleeping,
six deer jumped over a silvery stream.

While you were sleeping,
seven geese flew silently
past the moon,

and while you were sleeping,
eight rabbits played in a
misty meadow.

While you were sleeping, nine elephants
marched through the long grass,

and while you were sleeping,
ten penguins jumped out of the icy sea...

to join one hundred friends."

"Are they all sleeping now?" asked Daisy.
"I think so," said her mother. "And when you
go to bed tonight, they'll all wake up again."

"Then Little Owl should go to bed now," said Daisy as she tucked him in. "Sleep well, Little Owl," and she kissed his fluffy head.

Can you find

Daisy's ten penguins?